Always

MW01616403

by Gloria Ríos
illustrated by Nancy Cote

 HOUGHTON MIFFLIN HARCOURT
School Publishers

Printed in China

ISBN-13: 978-0-547-02726-5
ISBN-10: 0-547-02726-5

3 4 5 6 7 8 0940 18 17 16 15 14 13 12 11 10

People are always learning.
They start when they are just
babies.

Babies learn by exploring.
This baby studies her toys and
puts them in her mouth. When
the family dog comes near her,
she tries to learn about him, too!

2

Babies learn from their families. Lisa's mother reads books to her. Lisa looks at the pictures and listens to the stories. That helps her learn new words. Lisa tries to walk like her brother. She is happy to learn new things.

Older children learn in many **different** ways. Children can learn by playing. They learn how to do puzzles and how to play games. They learn to run and jump and climb. Hector has learned to use his arms and legs to climb up **high**.

Children need help to learn
some things. Parents teach them
how to tie their shoes. Teachers
teach children to read and write.

Hector's big sister can teach
him things, too. She is teaching
him how to ride a bicycle.

Teens learn how to do many things on their own.

Ana is old enough to do jobs to earn money. She also knows how to add and subtract in her head to be sure she gets the right change at stores.

Teens learn things that will help them live on their own someday. Many teens learn how to drive a car.

Teens learn in school, too. Ana's mother is always there to help her with her homework.

Adults know how to do many things. Ana's mother knows how to take care of a family. She knows how to use math at her job.

But she still learns from her dad. He taught her how to fix things around the house.

Grandparents are always learning, too. Some learn fun things like painting. Others learn helpful things like how to use a computer.

Hector and Ana's grandpa is learning something new. He hopes to master this new machine soon.

He doesn't give up. He asks for help. There are some very good teachers in his family! Once he gets help, he knows just what to do. He is sure that he can learn more each day. After all, people are ALWAYS learning!

Responding

✔ **TARGET SKILL** **Text and Graphic Features** Find two pictures from the story. How do they help you understand this story?
Make a chart.

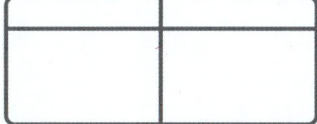

✏ Write About It

Text to Text What else have you read about people who are learning? When do you think people learn the most? Why? Write two sentences.

✔ **TARGET SKILL** **Text and Graphic Features** Tell how words work with art.

✔ **TARGET STRATEGY** **Analyze/Evaluate** Tell how you feel about the text, and why.

GENRE **Informational text** gives facts about a topic.